SQUIRRELS

Sally Morgan

FRANKLIN WATTS
LONDON • SYDNEY

© **2005 Franklin Watts**
First published in 2005
by Franklin Watts
96 Leonard Street
London EC2A 4XD

Franklin Watts Australia
45-51 Huntley Street
Alexandria NSW 2015

Produced for Franklin Watts by
White-Thomson Publishing Ltd
210 High Street
Lewes BN7 2NH

Editor: Rachel Minay
Designed by: Tinstar Design Ltd
Picture research: Morgan Interactive Ltd
Consultant: Frank Blackburn
Printed in: China

British Library Cataloguing
in Publication Data
A CIP catalogue record for this book is
available from the British Library.

ISBN: 0 7496 6065 1

Acknowledgements
The publishers would like to thank
the following for permission to
reproduce these photographs:

Corbis
6 (Gary Carter);

Ecoscene
4–5 (Alastair Shay), 9 (Ian Beames), 14
(Robin Redfern), 15 (Steve Austin), 16
(Robert Pickett), 17 (Frank Blackburn), 21
(Anthony Cooper), 23 (Malcolm Kitto), 29
(Peter Cairns);

Nature Picture Library
FC, 1 (Colin Varndell), 7 (Andrew Cooper),
8 (Mark Yates), 10 (Niall Benvie), 12
(Warwick Sloss), 13 (Mike Read), 18 (Peter
Cairns), 19 (Niall Benvie), 20 (Dietmar Nill),
22 (Tom Vezo), 24 (Colin Varndell), 25
(Niall Benvie), 26 (Georgette Douwma), 27
(Brian Lightfoot), 28 (Niall Benvie).

The map on page 11 was created by
Tinstar Design Ltd.

Every effort has been made to contact copyright
holders of any material reproduced in this book.
Any omissions will be rectified in subsequent
printings if notice is given to the publishers.

Contents

The squirrel

The squirrel is one of the best-known animals in Britain. It is a small animal with a bushy tail. Squirrels are very agile and live in trees.

ears

Red and grey squirrels

There are two species of squirrel living in Britain – the red squirrel and the grey squirrel. The red squirrel is the native squirrel that has lived in Britain for thousands of years. The grey squirrel was introduced from North America in 1876. It escaped from captivity and became wild. Soon it spread across the countryside, competing with the red squirrel for food. Today there are far more grey squirrels than red ones.

paws with
sharp claws

short front legs

long hind
(back) legs

animal CLUES

It is easy to tell the red squirrel from the grey. The red squirrel is smaller with reddish-brown hair and a bushy tail. The grey squirrel has a bushier tail, is heavier and has mostly grey hair. However, some grey squirrels have half-red, half-grey hair and a few are black.

Mammals

The squirrel is a mammal. Mammals typically give birth to live young, which they feed with milk from the female. The body of a mammal is usually covered with hair. Young squirrels are called kittens.

grey hair

tail

Reproduction

Squirrels can be seen courting in late winter when one or two chattering males chase a female through the trees. After mating, the male leaves the female and does not help to rear the young.

Kittens

The female squirrel is pregnant for about six weeks. Her kittens are usually born in March or April. She gives birth in a large nest, called a drey (see pages 22–23), in a tree.

ANIMAL FACTS

▶ *The kittens of the red squirrel weigh only 8–12 g at birth. Grey squirrel kittens weigh a little more, 10–15 g.*

These baby squirrels are only a few days old. As they do not have any hair, they huddle together to keep warm.

The kittens stay in the drey for seven weeks.

There are usually three or four kittens in a litter, but there may be as many as nine. The kittens are born without any hair or teeth. They are blind, deaf and completely dependent on their mother. She feeds them milk every three to four hours for the first few weeks.

The kittens' hair starts to grow after 10 days. By the time they are 21 days old the kittens are completely covered in hair. Their eyes and ears open after 30 days.

animal CLUES

The best time to see squirrels is in January and February when many trees have lost their leaves. This is when you can see the squirrels courting and hear them making screeching calls.

Growing up

When the kittens are about seven weeks old they are ready to follow their mother out of the drey onto the surrounding branches. By this time they look like smaller versions of adult squirrels.

Weaning

Now the kittens start weaning; they are ready to start eating some solid food. Their teeth have grown and they can chew food. By the time they are 10 weeks old they have been completely weaned.

Young squirrels chase up and down the trees, learning how to climb.

These young squirrels stay together as they explore the woodland.

Leaving mother

Young squirrels learn which foods to eat by watching their mother. They are ready to leave her when they are four months old. The young squirrels will stay close to their mother if there are not many squirrels living in the area. If there are lots of squirrels they will have to move further away. Having found somewhere to live, they have to build their own drey. These young squirrels will be ready to breed when they are one year old.

Often a female squirrel gives birth to a second litter in late June or July, after the kittens from her first litter have been weaned.

ANIMAL **FACTS**

▶ Between 50 and 75 per cent of squirrel kittens do not survive to their first birthday. Some are killed by predators, while others die from disease.

Living in the countryside

Squirrels are found in woodlands and trees that grow in hedgerows. Grey squirrels are found across Britain, whereas the red squirrel is only found in Scotland and Wales and parts of England. Red squirrels do not usually live in the same wood as grey squirrels.

Woodland homes

Woodland is a good habitat for squirrels. It is full of places to hide. The woods provide a lot of food that squirrels like to eat. Grey squirrels tend to prefer deciduous woodlands with oak and beech trees, whereas red squirrels prefer coniferous forests of pine and spruce.

Red squirrels do not usually live in deciduous woodlands, where oak and beech trees grow.

Red squirrels do not live as closely together as grey squirrels. Usually just one or two red squirrels live in 10,000 sq m of woodland, whereas there may be as many as nine grey squirrels living in 10,000 sq m.

Grey squirrels are found across England and Wales and in parts of Scotland. The red squirrel is found in Scotland and Wales and just a few places in England.

Red Squirrels

Grey Squirrels

ANIMAL **FACTS**

▶ *There are just over 160,000 red squirrels living in Britain, of which 30,000 are found in England. The British population of grey squirrels is 2,520,000. That means there are 16 grey squirrels for every one red squirrel.*

Living in cities

Grey squirrels have adapted well to town and city habitats, such as gardens and parks.

For a squirrel, there are many similarities between woodlands and cities. Woodlands are full of trees and there are many trees in parks and gardens. Walls and fences allow squirrels to move around a city with ease. There are plenty of places for squirrels to hide and they even find their way into roof spaces.

Grey squirrels are a common sight in city parks.

ANIMAL **FACTS**

▶ *Bird feeders are often sold as being 'squirrel proof'. They have extra bars to stop the squirrel from stealing the bird food.*

There is plenty of food for squirrels in cities too. The trees and shrubs produce a supply of fruits, nuts and seeds. Also, squirrels have learnt that people put out food for birds and bird food is good for squirrels! They are intelligent animals and soon learn how to steal nuts from most bird feeders. Some 'squirrel proof' bird feeders stop them though.

Grey squirrels can hang upside down on bird feeders to get at the food. This bird feeder has been designed to be 'squirrel proof'.

Squirrel food

Squirrels eat a variety of foods depending on the time of year. Their food includes hazelnuts, acorns, tree bark, fungi, buds, leaves, shoots and flowers. Frequently they raid birds' nests for eggs and young chicks.

Competing for food

Grey and red squirrels compete with each other for food. Grey squirrels eat a wide range of foods including the favourite foods of the red squirrel. Red squirrels do not eat such a variety of foods. If there is a shortage of food the red squirrels may starve. However, the grey squirrels survive because they can eat foods that red squirrels cannot, for example acorns, which come from oak trees. For this reason red and grey squirrels do not live in the same woodland for long and usually the red squirrels die out. Red squirrels survive for longer in woodlands where there are no oak trees.

This squirrel has found a nut to eat.

This pile of pine cones was left by a squirrel. You can see how some of the cones have been eaten down to the core.

Chisel-like teeth

Squirrels have large incisors at the front of their mouth that are ideal for breaking open nuts. These teeth grow continuously, as much as 12 cm each year. However, they stay short because the squirrel constantly wears them down by chewing on tough foods. Rats and mice have long incisors too.

ANIMAL **FACTS**

▶ *Lots of small mammals eat the seeds in pine cones. Once they have removed all the seeds they leave the discarded cones on the woodland floor. You can tell if a squirrel has eaten the seeds because it chews the cone right down to the core. It looks just like a chewed apple core!*

Squirrels have enemies

A wide variety of animals prey upon squirrels. These are animals such as birds of prey and larger mammals.

Predators

In cities, pet animals such as dogs and cats catch squirrels. In woodlands they are more likely to be preyed on by foxes and birds of prey such as buzzards. These birds swoop down onto the drey and take young kittens. Pine martens are found in northern coniferous woods. They are cat-like animals, related to stoats and weasels. They prey upon red squirrels.

The pine marten is an expert climber and can leap from branch to branch. It climbs into dreys to prey on young squirrels.

However, humans are the main enemy of the grey squirrel. Squirrels do a lot of damage to trees by gnawing the bark and this can kill young trees. Therefore foresters trap and shoot grey squirrels to protect the trees.

Food chains

A food chain is the feeding relationship between organisms. Plants are called producers. Animals that eat plants are called primary consumers. The squirrel is usually a primary consumer because it eats plant foods. Animals that eat primary consumers are called secondary consumers.

When the squirrel eats food produced by plants, it is classed as a primary consumer.

ANIMAL **FACTS**

▶ *In the 1830s it was very fashionable to wear a squirrel fur boa, which was a coil of fur that a woman wore around her neck. In 1839 alone, more than 2.7 million red squirrel skins were imported into Britain to make these fur boas.*

Movement

Squirrels are very agile animals. They can run along the narrowest of branches and leap from tree to tree.

Long hind legs

The skeleton of the squirrel is suited to climbing. The hind (back) legs of the squirrel are much longer than the front legs. Also they have powerful muscles in their hind legs. This means that they can leap considerable distances. The squirrel's bushy tail helps it to balance as it runs along branches and acts as a rudder when it jumps.

A squirrel can run along narrow branches, gripping with its claws and using its tail for balance.

Squirrels grip with their claws
as they run down tree trunks.

Running down
tree trunks

Squirrels can run down tree
trunks head first just as easily
as they can climb up them.
They have sharp claws to
grip the bark. When they
run down a tree trunk the
claws of their hind feet
stick into the bark,
acting as an
anchor to stop
the squirrel
from falling
off the tree.

Senses

Squirrels need good eyesight to avoid predators. Their ability to judge distances means they can leap from tree to tree. They need other senses such as smell to find food.

Seeing

The squirrel has large round eyes, which are positioned towards the front of its head. It is particularly good at seeing vertical objects and it can estimate the distance between trees with great accuracy. This means that squirrels can jump safely. Eyesight is important when looking out for predators such as foxes and pine martens.

ANIMAL **FACTS**

▶ *Before a squirrel buries a nut, it breaks the shell with its teeth and cleans it by licking or rubbing it on its face. This cleaning is thought to smear a scent over the nut to help the squirrel find it again.*

Squirrels can judge distances so they leap safely from branch to branch.

The squirrel holds its food in its paws and smells it before eating.

Smell and touch

Squirrels use their sense of smell when feeding. They choose between good and bad nuts by holding the nuts in their paws, weighing then smelling them. Also, they use smell to find food that they have buried in the ground (see page 26). A squirrel's sense of touch is well developed, too. It has long, touch-sensitive whiskers around its nose and on its feet.

science LINKS

We don't have whiskers like a squirrel, but our skin is very sensitive. We can detect hot and cold, pressure and pain. Different areas of the skin are more sensitive than others. For example, your fingertips are one of the most sensitive areas of your skin. Try touching different areas of skin on your arm to find the most sensitive and the least sensitive.

Squirrel homes

The squirrel has two types of home. One is called a den and the other is a drey.

Dens

The den is a hollow space, lined with leaves and grass, in a tree. It is used as a temporary home. Squirrels sleep in the den and take shelter in it during bad weather.

ANIMAL **FACTS**

▶ *A well-built drey may last for two or three years, through wind, rain and storms.*

Dreys

The drey is a larger and more permanent home. It is a nest about 50 cm across and built high in a tree. It is made of twigs and lined with dry grass, shredded bark, moss and feathers.

This grey squirrel is carrying twigs and leaves back to its drey.

A drey looks just like a large messy bird's nest.

Dreys have to be carefully positioned. If a drey is built on the outside of the tree it may be exposed to rain and get wet. Dreys built in the middle of the tree are sheltered and are less likely to be shaken or blown apart in strong winds.

Squirrels build a number of dreys and swap from one to another every few days. This means that if one is damaged the squirrel has other dreys to use.

animal CLUES

Winter is a good time to see dreys in trees. A drey is usually in the middle of the tree, often in a fork between branches. It looks like a large pile of twigs.

Communication

Squirrels communicate with each other by signalling with their tails, and through sounds and smell.

Twitching tails

Tails are very important to squirrels as they use them to communicate with each other. They twitch their tails if they are uneasy or suspicious. This can mean 'stay away' to another squirrel.

The grey squirrel has a large tail that can be seen from a distance by other squirrels.

Calling to each other

Grey squirrels make a wide range of calls. When a squirrel is agitated it makes a *chuk-chuk* sound. If a squirrel sees a predator it produces an alarm call. This alarm call warns other squirrels of approaching danger.

Smell

Smell is also important. A squirrel's favourite routes through the trees are marked with its urine. This is a message to other squirrels to keep away. Squirrels identify each other by smell too.

ANIMAL **FACTS**

▶ *Grey squirrels can be quite aggressive at certain times of the year, especially during the breeding season. When squirrels fight, they roll or tumble along the ground in close bodily contact. Often this results in injuries to the head, shoulders, back and ears.*

This red squirrel has spotted something. It will alert other squirrels by making an alarm call.

Surviving winter

Many small mammals spend the winter asleep in a warm dry place. Squirrels do not, as they cannot survive long without food. They are active all through winter, coming out each day to find food.

Preparing for winter

During the autumn squirrels are busy collecting food, especially seeds and nuts. They eat a lot of food so that they put on weight.

There will be little food for them in winter so they bury seeds in the ground. When they are hungry in winter they search out their stores of seeds. Most squirrels bury enough seeds to provide food for up to 50 days.

Seeds fall to the ground in autumn and squirrels collect them to store. This grey squirrel is collecting sweet chestnuts that have fallen to the ground.

science LINKS

Often the squirrels do not find their buried stores and the seeds germinate in the ground. In order to germinate, a seed needs water, air and often warmth. Many have to be in the dark too. Tree seeds such as acorns and hazelnuts need to experience a period of cold before they can germinate. This ensures that the seeds germinate in spring rather than in autumn when they fall from the trees.

Winter dreys

Squirrels use one of their dreys in winter. The chosen drey is built up with twigs so that it is extra-thick and very warm. A squirrel spends much of the winter in its drey, just coming out to search for its stores of hidden food. Sometimes it shares its winter drey with other squirrels. When the squirrel sleeps, it curls its tail around its body to act as a blanket.

Squirrel stories

Hard winter ahead?

Some people believe that if squirrels collect and bury lots of nuts in autumn, the winter will be long and hard. Other people say that the squirrels collect lots of nuts if there is a bumper crop of nuts and that it has nothing to do with the weather! Some people believe that another sign of a cold winter ahead is when squirrels have extra-thick tails or if they build larger dreys.

Tails for sails

People have often wondered how squirrels manage to cross stretches of water to reach islands. In *The Tale of Squirrel Nutkin* by Beatrix Potter, the red squirrels cross to the island on rafts made from old bits of wood that float on the water. They stick their tails in the air to catch the wind, just like sails.

Squirrel facts

Squirrel family

Squirrels are a type of rodent. Rodents have a chisel-shaped incisor tooth at the front of their mouth for chewing. There are 27 different species or types of squirrel, including chipmunks, ground squirrels and marmots.

Tall tails

Part of the Latin name for the squirrel, *Sciurus*, comes from a Greek word that means 'shade tail'. This comes from the squirrel's habit of sitting upright with its bushy tail held up behind it, shading it from the sun.

MAIN FEATURES OF THE SQUIRREL

- *Squirrels are mammals.*
- *Squirrels are rodents.*
- *Red and grey squirrels have long back legs for jumping.*
- *Their young are called kittens.*
- *They live in dens and dreys.*
- *Squirrels do not hibernate in winter.*

Squirrel websites

Red squirrels
www.snh.org.uk
A website featuring information about red squirrels in Scotland.

Grey squirrels
www.british-wildlife.com/animals/greysquirrel.htm
Features information about grey squirrels and other wildlife around Britain.

Note to parents and teachers
Every effort has been made by the publishers to ensure that these websites are suitable for children; that they are of the highest educational value, and that they contain no inappropriate or offensive material. However, because of the nature of the Internet, it is impossible to guarantee that the contents of these sites will not be altered. We strongly advise that Internet access is supervised by a responsible adult.

Glossary

adapt get used to

agile able to move quickly and easily

bird of prey a predatory bird, such as an eagle, osprey or falcon, that has a hooked beak and powerful claws

captivity kept in a zoo or wildlife park, not allowed to roam free

coniferous a coniferous tree has needles rather than leaves, for example the pine and spruce

courting behaviour leading up to mating

deciduous a deciduous tree drops its leaves in winter, for example the oak and beech

drey the nest of a squirrel

food chain feeding relationships between different organisms, for example seeds are eaten by squirrels and squirrels are eaten by foxes

germinate start growing (of a seed)

habitat the place where an animal lives

incisor a narrow-edged tooth at the front of the mouth

mammal an animal that usually gives birth to live young. The female mammal produces milk for her young

mate reproduce

native person or animal that has lived in a particular place for a long time

population the number of individuals living in a certain area, for example the number of squirrels living in a wood or the number of fish in a pond

predator an animal that hunts other animals

pregnant a female animal is pregnant when she has a baby or babies developing inside her

prey on/upon hunt

rudder flat piece of wood or metal fixed to the back of a boat, used for steering

urine the water passed out of the body of an animal

weaning changing a baby animal from a milk diet to foods eaten by adult animals

Index